MAKING A DIFFERENCE

Janet Coburn

Contents

A Harcourt Achieve Imprint

www.Rigby.com
1-800-531-5015

Vivien Thomas: Talented Hands

When Vivien Thomas was a young man, all the African American carpenter wanted to do was work hard and make an honest living for his family. Vivien's brother, Harold, however, had other dreams. Harold was a schoolteacher who strongly believed in **civil rights** and felt it was unfair that Caucasian teachers received more money than African American teachers. Harold made a difference by helping to change the laws about teachers' pay. What Vivien didn't know then was that he, too, would make a difference and in turn help people of all races.

Vivien Thomas

Vivien Thomas was born in 1910 near Lake Providence, Louisiana. While he was still young, his family moved to Nashville, Tennessee. At that time, Nashville was a growing city in the southern United States that had colleges, museums, banks, and many businesses and industries. Nashville had a need for carpenters to build houses, buildings, and places of business.

Thomas became a skilled carpenter who could carve and shape small pieces of wood that fit together in beautiful patterns. This type of carpentry, called inlay, was difficult to do well and should have earned Thomas high pay and steady work.

Inlay carpentry is very unique. It takes a skilled craftsman to create it.

Vivien spent his early years in Nashville, Tennessee.

During the Great Depression many people lost their homes. They built shelters using anything they could find.

Nashville, however, began to suffer from hard times in the late 1920s. Banks and businesses suddenly closed, and workers like Thomas lost their jobs and their savings. Nashville was not the only city hurt by these events; people across the United States had the same problems. It was the beginning of a difficult time called the Great Depression.

The Great Depression was hard for everyone. Entire families moved across the United States in search of jobs. Finding jobs and getting paid well had never been easy for African American families, and during the Great Depression, they were lucky to get any work at all.

Vivien in 1929

Vivien had been searching for a job for a long time when finally a surgeon named Alfred Blalock hired Vivien to help him in his laboratory. Dr. Blalock worked with sick dogs so he could learn how to help sick people. His lab had a kennel that was full of sick dogs recovering from operations who needed their bandages changed and cleaned. Vivien cared for the dogs and cleaned the medical equipment as carefully as he had inlaid beautiful designs in wood floors. There was a bonus to the job, too. There were many medical books in the lab, and Vivien enjoyed reading them. He had always dreamed of going to medical school.

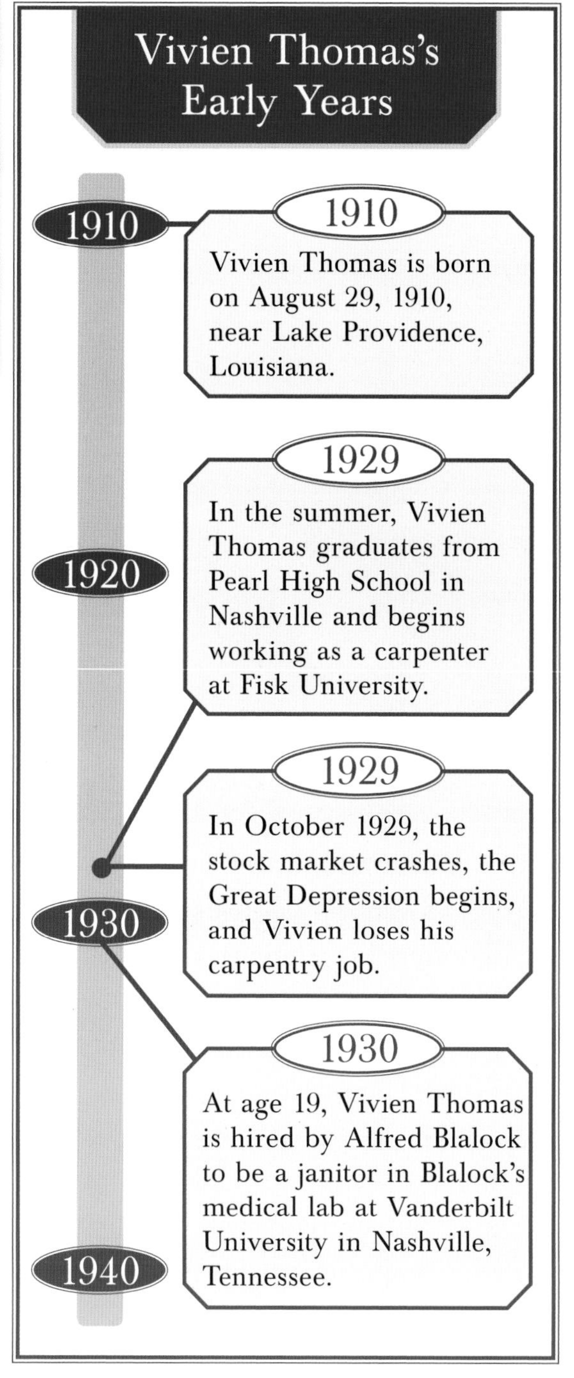

A Partnership Begins

Dr. Blalock noticed what a good worker Thomas was. He realized that Thomas had a good memory, was eager to learn, and had skillful hands. Thomas could handle delicate glass tubes without breaking them, and he could work on old machines and make them run better.

Blalock began letting Thomas help him during the operations. Thomas read Blalock's medical books and took many notes about the operations. His skillful fingers tied off tiny **sutures**, or threads. Without ever going to medical school, Thomas was receiving a medical education.

Dr. Alfred Blalock

Dr. Blalock and his surgical team performing a surgery.

When a person is severely injured, his or her body may go into shock. Shock, or trauma, was a medical problem that doctors did not know how to treat in the 1930s. Even if doctors were able to sew up all the cuts and set the broken bones, many patients would still die. Dr. Blalock thought that loss of blood might be what caused people to go into shock, but simply giving a person more blood did not seem to help.

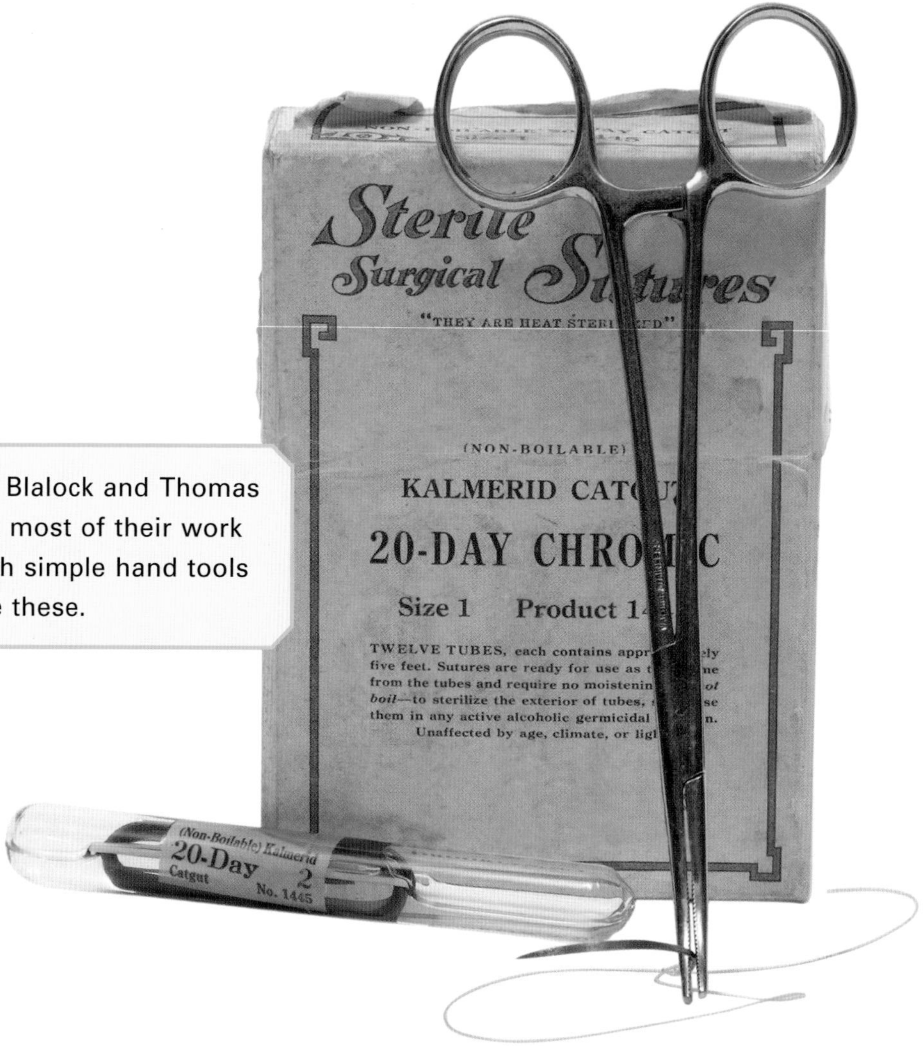

Dr. Blalock and Thomas did most of their work with simple hand tools like these.

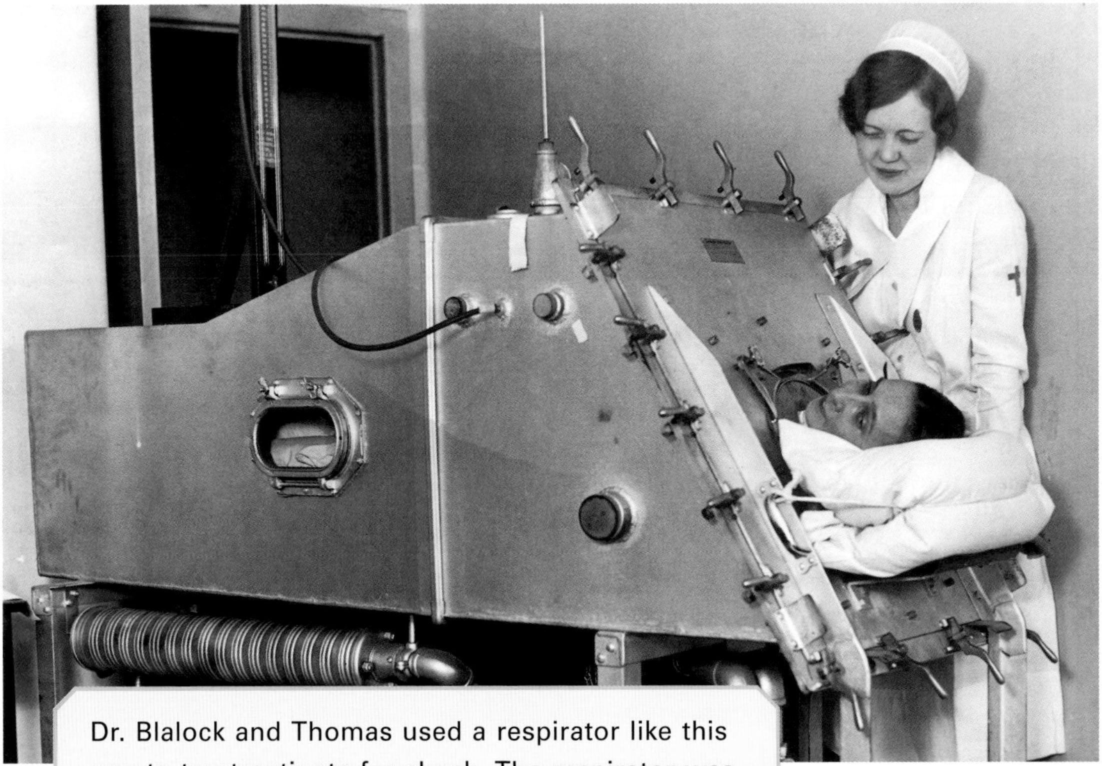

Dr. Blalock and Thomas used a respirator like this one to treat patients for shock. The respirator was invented in 1927 and is nicknamed the "iron lung."

Dr. Blalock and Thomas came up with the idea that lack of oxygen might cause shock, and Thomas worked very hard to come up with a solution for this problem. One day Dr. Blalock noticed Thomas working on an old machine that had been lying around the lab. "What on Earth is that?" the doctor asked.

"It's our new respirator," Thomas replied. He showed Dr. Blalock how the simple pump could push air into a dog's lungs. He thought maybe it could help people breathe, too. The respirator would help the patient's body add oxygen to the blood while the doctor sewed up cuts and treated heavy bleeding. This would help keep the person from going into shock.

Coming up with the solution of using a respirator when helping people in shock made Dr. Blalock very famous. Until then, he had been just another scientist. Suddenly he was popular and important. Large medical schools and hospitals began offering Dr. Blalock jobs to teach, heal, or research any subject of his choosing.

Blalock knew that he could not have solved the problem without Thomas, and in order to continue doing groundbreaking work, he needed his great assistant. When some schools or hospitals would not offer Thomas a position there, too, Blalock turned them down. In 1941 Dr. Blalock finally accepted an offer from Johns Hopkins Medical School in Baltimore, Maryland, because they agreed to give Thomas a position as well.

Johns Hopkins Medical School in Baltimore, Maryland, was one of the finest medical schools anywhere. Dr. Blalock was honored to serve as chief of surgery there.

Johns Hopkins was one of the most famous and important teaching hospitals in the world, but many members of the staff did not think Thomas should be Dr. Blalock's lab manager because he was African American. At that time, all of the African American workers at Johns Hopkins were cooks or janitors, not managers. The administrators allowed Dr. Blalock to bring Thomas along, but Thomas was paid the same as a janitor, even though he was inventing new medical devices and helping with operations.

Like his brother Harold, Vivien believed that it was unfair that he received janitor's pay for doing a lab manager's job. Many of the doctors and other lab managers did not respect Thomas and treated him badly.

Vivien was frustrated and felt he deserved to be treated fairly. He could have gone to medical school and become a doctor instead of going to Johns Hopkins with Dr. Blalock. Vivien was smart, hardworking, and excellent at what he did. His skills were very valuable to Dr. Blalock, and Blalock could not afford to lose Vivien as an assistant.

In the 1940s, many people were surprised to see Vivien Thomas in his white medical lab jacket at Johns Hopkins.

In the 1940s, life was hard for African Americans. They had not yet begun to have the freedoms and opportunities that people like Martin Luther King, Jr., would later fight for.

Dr. Blalock tried to make things right, and he finally convinced the people at Johns Hopkins that Thomas was a great lab manager and should earn more than a janitor's salary. Thomas finally received equal pay, but Dr. Blalock could not change everything.

Johns Hopkins was a **segregated** hospital, where Caucasians and African Americans still had to use separate restrooms and drinking fountains. Thomas had to enter the hospital through a door used only for African Americans.

Blue Baby Syndrome

At Johns Hopkins, Dr. Blalock worked with a pediatric cardiologist named Helen Taussig. Dr. Blalock and Dr. Taussig studied a condition called a congenital heart defect, or "blue baby syndrome." A "blue baby" is born with a heart that is not able to supply blood to the lungs correctly. When the lungs do not supply enough oxygen for the baby, the baby's skin turns blue. Without enough oxygen in his or her body, the baby can die.

Most doctors at the time believed that it was too dangerous to operate on the human heart, and operating on a baby's heart was even more unthinkable. Who could possibly work on such a tiny heart, lungs, and veins?

Dr. Blalock, Dr. Taussig, and Thomas worked for two years to find a way to get more oxygen to a "blue baby's" damaged heart and lungs. Finally Dr. Taussig came up with the idea to join a healthy blood vessel from the heart to the lungs. Thomas practiced the surgery on dogs with the same defect until he could sew the tiny blood vessels without even looking.

Dr. Helen Taussig was the first woman to serve as President of the American Heart Association. She also received the Presidential Medal of Freedom from President Lyndon Baines Johnson.

In 1944 Dr. Blalock and Thomas were ready to operate on a human baby. Because Thomas was not a doctor, he could only watch Dr. Blalock perform the surgery, but Thomas's successful experiences of operating on dogs was **invaluable** to Blalock. Crowds of doctors gathered to watch Thomas guide Dr. Blalock though the operation. It was a success and the baby lived!

Thomas performed open-heart surgery on this dog. Her name was Anna, and this picture of her hangs in the rotunda at Johns Hopkins University with Thomas's picture. It is the only portrait in the rotunda that is not of a human.

Solving a Problem

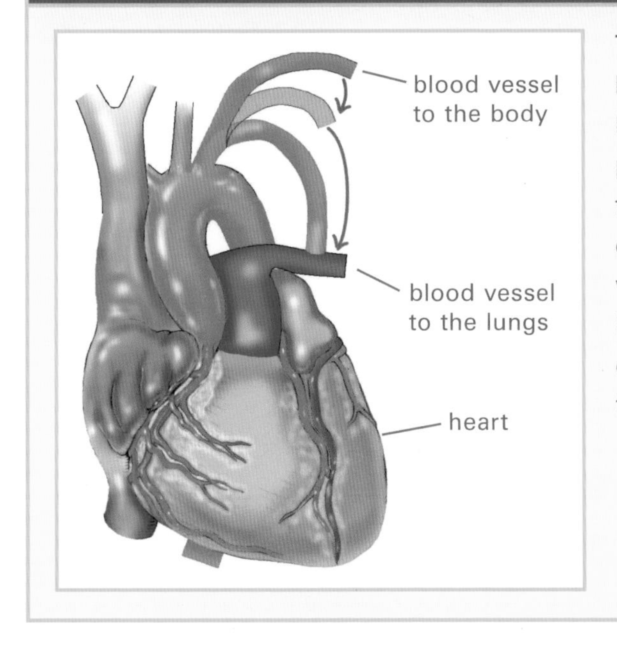

Thomas, Dr. Blalock, and Dr. Taussig fixed the Blue Baby problem by taking part of the blood vessel that goes to the body and connecting it to the blood vessel that goes to the lungs so that the blood could go back to the lungs for oxygen.

In the year following the successful operation, Thomas, Blalock, and Taussig performed more than 200 similiar operations and, since that first "blue baby" operation, millions of babies have been saved. Dr. Blalock became famous for being brave enough to try the new operation and for succeeding. Thomas went on to teach many young doctors how to perform the operation, even though he was still just a lab manager.

Symptoms of Blue Baby Syndrome

A child with Blue Baby Syndrome has four problems with his/her heart:

- The opening of the blood vessel that goes to the lungs gets smaller.
- There is a hole in the heart's wall that separates the left and right chambers. It causes the blood with oxygen to mix with the blood that has no oxygen.
- Because of the hole and the smaller opening of the blood vessel, the right wall has to work harder, causing it to get too big.
- To make up for these problems, the blood vessel to the body begins to take over, causing the hole to get bigger.

All of these problems mean that a person's blood does not get enough oxygen.

In 1976 Johns Hopkins honored Thomas with the title of Doctor. His painting now hangs in the beautiful rotunda where he once was not allowed to enter. His discoveries have helped save millions of lives and have made a difference for millions of families.

Johns Hopkins created the Vivien Thomas Fund to allow other young people the chance to study medicine, the American Heart Association offers a Vivien Thomas Young Investigator Award for young doctors, and the Morehouse School of Medicine has a Vivien Thomas Research Program for high school students. Dr. Thomas died in 1985, but his work is still making a difference today.

In 1976 Vivien Thomas received the title of Doctor from Johns Hopkins for all his hard work. He was a valuable member of the staff from 1941 to 1985.

Jimmy Carter: A Life of Public Service

Jimmy Carter, the 39th President of the United States, has always believed in human rights and has worked to end suffering around the world. As president he did many important things to right **injustices**, and after his presidency he worked even harder to make a difference in his community and the world.

James Earl Carter, born on October 1, 1924, in Plains, Georgia, was the son of a farmer and a nurse. He grew up in the small town of Archery, Georgia, with one brother and two sisters. As a child he enjoyed reading, and as he grew up, he became a local football and basketball star at Plains High School.

When he was 22, Jimmy finished college and received his degree from the United States Naval Academy. After college he married Rosalynn Smith and entered the United States Navy where he served on submarines.

He returned home from the Navy in 1953 after the death of his father and took over the family peanut farming business. While farming he and Rosalynn raised their four children. Jimmy also became involved in local and state politics where he felt he could make a difference.

While in the Navy, Jimmy used his knowledge of nuclear physics and reactor technology to become a nuclear engineer.

President James Earl Carter

A New President

Jimmy announced he was running for President of the United States on December 12, 1974. The election was two years away, and nobody thought that Jimmy could win. Jimmy wanted to use the presidency to help others, so he traveled all over the United States to let the people know that he would be sensitive to their needs and capable of meeting their expectations. The people believed he could do a good job and elected him President of the United States on November 2, 1976. He took the Oath of Office and was sworn in as president on January 20, 1977.

Jimmy Carter was the son of a peanut farmer who became President of the United States by defeating Gerald Ford in the 1976 presidential election. He received 297 electoral votes to Ford's 241.

In 1979 President Carter helped Egyptian President Anwar Sadat and Israeli Prime Minister Menachem Begin reach a peace agreement.

During his time as president from 1977 to 1981, Jimmy did many great things. He raised awareness for saving electricity by installing solar panels on the roof of the White House and using a wood stove to heat it. He encouraged the countries of Israel and Egypt to make a peaceful agreement and created 103 million acres of new national park land in Alaska. Through all of this, his main goal was to further the cause of equal rights for all people all around the world.

After the Presidency

On January 20, 1981, Ronald Reagan was sworn in as the 40th President of the United States, and Jimmy Carter left the White House as a private citizen to continue his life of public service. Most former presidents write books and make speeches, but Jimmy was different. He knew there were still millions of people around the world who were suffering. He wanted to work to help make other people's lives better.

Jimmy and Rosalynn tour an Ethiopian village where the Carter Center has worked to stop trachoma, an eye disease that can cause blindness.

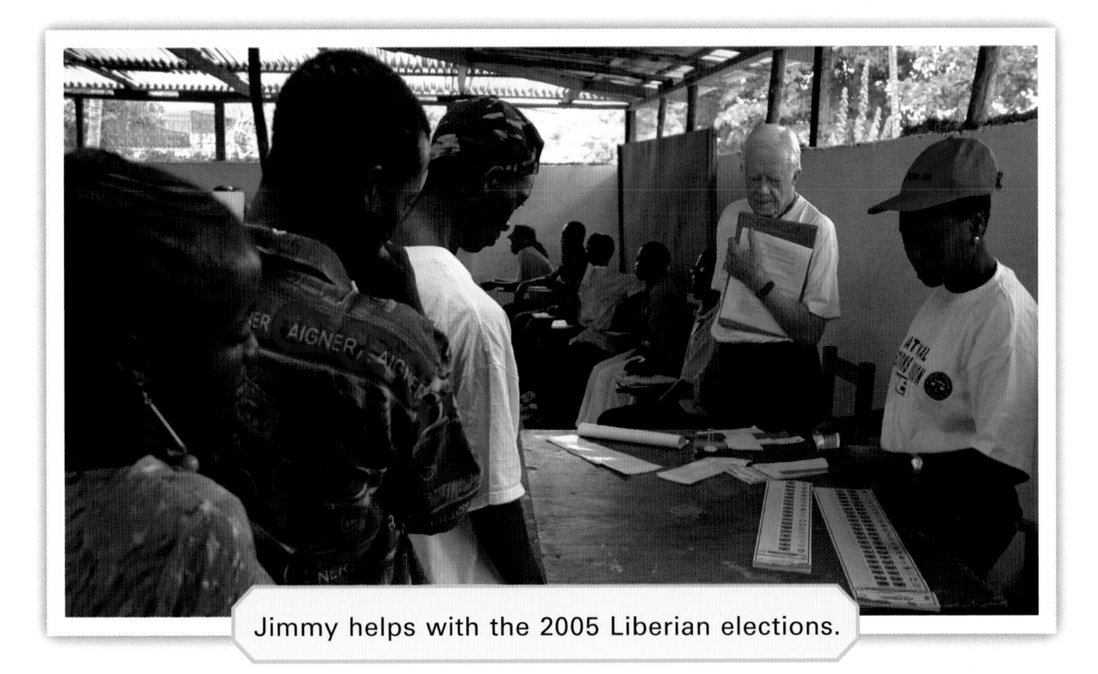
Jimmy helps with the 2005 Liberian elections.

In 1982 with Rosalynn's help, Jimmy founded the Carter Center in Atlanta, Georgia. The Carter Center's goal is to work to end human suffering and improve the quality of life for people all around the world.

Since his presidency, through his work at the Carter Center, Jimmy has helped **promote** peace by helping world leaders discuss ways to end conflicts. He has also supported **democracy** around the world by helping to monitor world elections to ensure fairness. The center also works to support good health care for people around the world. It is the center's and Jimmy's belief that every human has the right to a healthy, happy life and a good clean home.

While the Carter Center focuses on helping people around the world, Jimmy knew that there were people at home that needed his help. He knew that more than 30 million U.S. families had housing problems, including high costs, overcrowding, and a lack of hot water or electricity. He also knew that more than 5 million people in the United States lived in poverty. Jimmy wanted to help people get out of poverty and own their own homes, so he found an organization he could work for that did just that.

Housing Trouble in the United States

Many people in the United States do not have decent places to live. Many families are forced to live in crowded, unsafe houses. Buying a house or paying rent can also be difficult for many people to afford. There is a great need for good, affordable housing in the United States.

Volunteer workers have helped Habitat for Humanity build more than 200,000 homes around the world, giving more than 1,000,000 people a safe place to live.

Habitat for Humanity is an organization that works to end poor housing and homelessness by building good houses for those who need them. It was immediately clear that Habitat for Humanity was an organization that shared the former president's belief in working to help others, and in 1984 Jimmy and Rosalynn began working with Habitat for Humanity.

How Habitat for Humanity Works

The Habitat for Humanity staff runs independent, local groups who raise the money, build the houses, select the families, and keep the projects going. Each local group also gives 10 percent of the money it raises to help Habitat for Humanity in other countries. There are more than 2,100 groups in all 50 U.S. states and more than 100 in other countries.

Habitat for Humanity does not just give away their houses. Future homeowners take some of the responsibility in building their houses. That way they can be proud to live in a home that they helped create.

This family helped build their new home.

Each family pays $500, works 300–500 hours helping to build the home, and makes monthly payments after they move into their home. These monthly payments are not rent; the money goes toward helping to build more houses. The people actually own the home after it is built.

Habitat for Humanity continues to grow every day with over ten different sub-programs. One new sub-program is called Women Build, which trains women to build houses and use tools they might not have worked with before. Girls Build is another exciting part of Habitat for Humanity that teaches 10–12 year old girls about homes, neighborhoods, home buying, building, and Habitat for Humanity. When they are old enough, some girls help to build houses with Habitat for Humanity, or at the very least, they learn about how to make a difference.

Habitat for Humanity has also taught young people from around the world about housing problems and how to help solve them. Young people from Paraguay, the Czech Republic, Bolivia, and Guyana have toured areas where Habitat for Humanity is building homes. When young people return home, they are able to join or start Habitat for Humanity groups of their own.

Women volunteers build about 150 new homes each year. All-women crews have built more than 800 homes!

During their first project in 1984, the Carters and other volunteers traveled 24 hours on a bus from Georgia to New York City to help rebuild a 6-story building that was home to 19 families. The project was a huge success.

Now the Carters choose a Jimmy Carter Work Project every year. They do special projects all over the United States and around the world. In 2002, the Jimmy Carter Work Project built 1,000 houses in 18 countries in Africa.

Having a former U.S. president involved with Habitat for Humanity has made more people aware of the group and their good work. Jimmy has even appeared on popular television shows to help people become aware of the work Habitat for Humanity does.

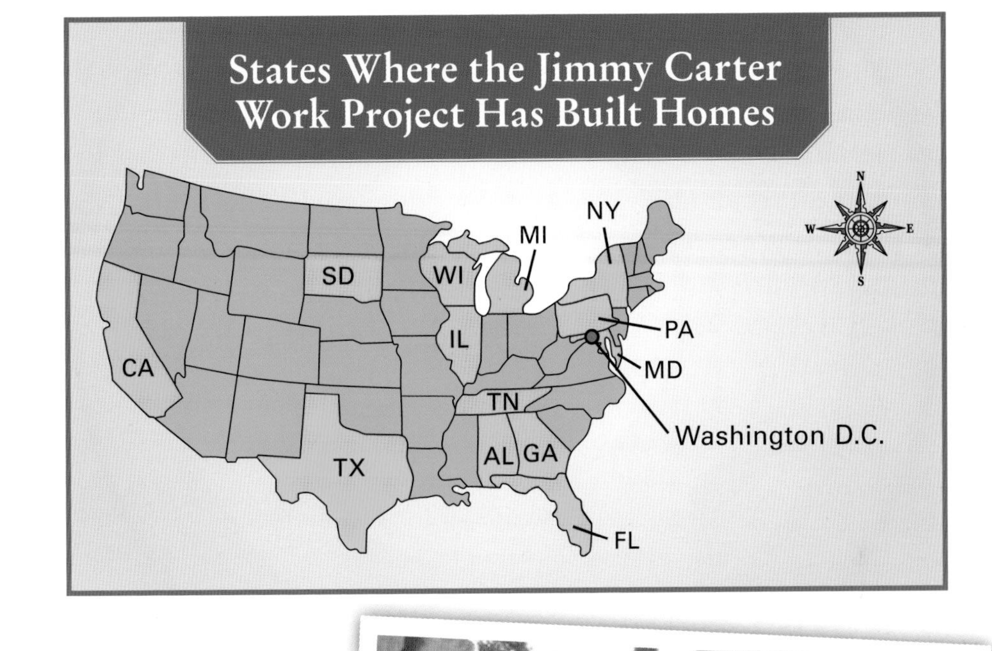

Jimmy is a skilled carpenter. In fact, his White House staff gave him carpentry tools once as a gift.

Jimmy accomplished many important things as President of the United States, and he has accomplished even more since he left office. He has received over 35 awards and honors for this work, including the Presidential Medal of Freedom in 1999 and the Nobel Peace Prize in 2002. He has been given over 15 honorary degrees from different universities. He has also found time to write 20 books, one of which is a historical fiction novel. It is the first fiction book to be written by a United States president.

Jimmy was honored with the Nobel Peace Prize for his unending efforts to promote peace, democracy, and human rights.

Jimmy was the only president to serve on a submarine. In 1998 this submarine was named the *USS Jimmy Carter.*

Whether he was working as President of the United States, a Habitat for Humanity volunteer, or a peanut farmer, Jimmy Carter has worked his whole life to make the world a better place. He is one man who has definitely made a difference.

Through his hard work and dedication, Jimmy Carter has made the world a better place for many people.

Craig Kielburger: Children for Children

Meet Craig Kielburger, a young Canadian boy. He enjoys watching television, playing soccer and video games, and running with his dog, Muffin. But when Craig Kielburger was 12, his life changed—all because he picked up a newspaper to look for the comics section.

When he picked up the newspaper, Craig noticed a picture on the front page. It showed a boy from Pakistan named Iqbal Masih. No one really knew the boy's age, but everyone thought he was around 12—just like Craig. The story told how Iqbal had been shot and killed while riding his bicycle because he had been speaking out against **child labor**.

Iqbal Masih's life had been nothing like Craig's. At the age of four, Iqbal was sold to people who owned a carpet factory. He was forced to work long hours, six days a week, and he was fined for any mistakes he made. Finally at age ten, Iqbal escaped from the factory. He traveled with human rights groups, told people how difficult the lives of child workers were, and explained why child labor was wrong.

Iqbal Masih

Iqbal's story worried Craig. He had never heard about child labor before, but he gathered his friends and started to learn more about it.

Craig Kielburger

Craig and his group of friends wanted to learn more about child labor. While researching, they discovered that there are 250 million child workers around the world. These children make very little money, and business owners sometimes keep them locked up. Most child workers have gone to school for only a year or two, and once they begin working, they have no more time for school.

This is Free The Children's official logo. It represents children helping children around the world through education. They have helped provide more than 400 schools to more than 35,000 children around the world.

Beautiful carpets like these might make thousands of dollars for a carpet seller. Free The Children wanted to know what happened to the children like Iqbal who actually made the rug.

Craig's group saw that too many people bought products without thinking about how much suffering went into making them. The children who work in carpet factories often have trouble breathing from the dust and fibers in the air, and their fingers become stiff and sore from tying the tiny knots. They can also suffer growth and bone problems from bending over a loom all day.

Craig and his friends asked the Canadian government to label rugs made in other countries. That way people could be sure they were not buying carpets made by child workers like Iqbal Masih.

In 1995 Craig Kielburger and his friends started an organization called Free The Children. They held bake sales, car washes, and garage sales, and all of the money they made went toward making people aware of child labor and finding ways to help child workers. Free The Children is still making a difference today.

Craig and his friends in Free The Children also gave speeches and wrote letters to help stop child labor. After a year, Craig's mother saw how much work he had taken on. Worried that it was too much for such a young boy, she told him to quit and get back to a normal life. Craig told his mother that fighting child labor had become his mission. When she saw how important it was for him to make a difference, she supported his efforts.

Craig thought that in order to speak honestly about the problem of child labor he should travel to meet some of the child workers themselves.

Craig wanted to travel and meet some child workers and see the places where they worked. The trip would cost a lot of money, so he asked friends and relatives for money instead of Christmas and birthday presents. He took on odd jobs, took money from his savings, and even sold a valuable set of hockey trading cards! Craig also wrote letters to families and groups asking them to help him. Finally he had saved enough money.

Free The Children has been in business since 1995, and it is growing bigger all the time. Craig's involvement has been key to FTC's success.

A Firsthand Look

Craig and his older friend Alam Rahman visited child workers, factories, shops, and farms in Thailand, Bangladesh, India, Nepal, and Pakistan. He met an eight-year-old girl whose job was to take apart used plastic syringes. Used syringes can carry deadly diseases, and if she stepped on a syringe or stuck herself with one, washing in dirty water was the only medical care she would receive.

Craig met other children who worked baking bricks, carrying heavy bags, driving rickshaws, and doing other difficult jobs for as many as 17 hours each day. Many of these children had no homes and earned little or no money.

There are over 250 million child workers around the world.

Since his first trip, Craig has traveled to many more countries representing Free the Children as an international child rights activist. This organization was nominated for the Nobel Peace Prize in 2002, 2003, and 2004.

Craig did not speak the same languages as the children he met, but some of the children knew a little English. His friend Alam also translated for him. In spite of the language difficulties, Craig got to know some of the children. Children in India tried to teach him a local game called *carom* and laughed when they saw him try to play badminton. They enjoyed his stories about snowball fights and maple syrup season in Canada.

Craig was deeply touched when he saw freed child workers join their families in small villages like this one. Some children had not been home for years.

While Craig was in India, a human rights group planned to free the children working in a carpet factory. Alam was afraid that the factory owners would learn of the plan and hide the children away before they could be rescued, but his fear did not come true. The group was able to free many child workers; however, the factory owner escaped.

Craig went with some of the rescued boys as they returned to their homes and villages. As they drove along, the boys sang in Hindi, "We are free!"

During his trip, Craig visited a center that helps children who have escaped slavery. At the center, these children receive medical care and an education, but most of all, they learn that they are good people who deserved a better life.

Craig was there on a day when some of the children graduated from the center. There was a big party, and each child talked about life as a child worker. Every child ended their story by saying, “Now I am free.”

Making Progress

During a trip to Southeast Asia, Craig learned that Jean Chrétien, the Prime Minister of Canada at that time, would be visiting Asia at the same time. Craig hoped to meet with Chrétien and talk to him about child labor during his trip, but Chrétien said he was too busy.

Craig held a press conference where he told of the miseries and hardships of child labor. Newspapers all over Canada covered the event and Craig got a lot of attention. Five days later, Chrétien's office called Craig to set up a meeting.

Craig Kielburger was able to get a private meeting with Canadian Prime Minister Jean Chrétien. Craig believes Canada can make a big difference for children's rights.

During the meeting, Craig reminded Chrétien that Canada was a world leader in human rights and should speak out against child labor. At first Craig did not think he was getting through to the Prime Minister, but in the end, Chrétien agreed to talk about the problem of child labor in his speeches and talks.

By continuing to speak out, Craig has spread his message about child labor and helped many children around the world.

Free The Children is still fighting to end child labor. They empower children by helping them make a difference in the lives of other children around the world.

Because Craig feels so strongly that this is an issue for children, many members of the Board of Directors are younger than 18. He wants to allow children to tell their stories in their own voices. There are many **charitable** organizations that are run by adults. Free The Children is an organization run by children for children.

In 2006, Craig traveled to the Massai Mara region of Kenya as a part of a team for the Schoolbuilding program.

How Does Free The Children Help?

Free The Children has initiated four Education for All programs targeted at bringing about social change.

- **Schoolbuilding**—This program focuses on building primary schools in Kenya, Sierra Leone, rural China, and Sri Lanka. Many youth volunteers get to help on site.
- **Alternative Income**—This program helps families find other ways to provide income so their children can go to school instead of work.
- **Health Care, Water and Sanitation**—This program helps children get proper health care to stay healthy.
- **Peacebuilding**—This program works to create a safe and peaceful environment for children who have been affected by war.

In 1995 Craig Kielburger and 11 friends started what would become Free The Children. Now Free The Children is the largest network of children helping children with more than a million youth volunteers around the world in more than 45 countries. There are more than 700 Youth in Action Groups working together with adult volunteers to raise money and awareness for the education and support of children in need. The Free The Children volunteers demonstrate that anyone who is willing to make a difference can bring about positive social change.

Craig Kielburger told the story of his trip to Southeast Asia in this book. He has since written other books about Free The Children and its mission.

Craig Kielburger is now an adult member on the board of Free The Children and also still works with the group by writing books, giving speeches, and helping them raise money. He hopes to continue to find ways to spread peace around the world and plans to work until all children are free.

Free The Children shows that children can be a powerful force for good in the world, and Craig has proven that you don't have to be a famous world leader, or even an adult, to make a difference in people's lives.

Craig wants children to know that they can speak out and make a difference about ideas they care about.

Glossary

charitable generous to others

child labor using children under the legal age as workers

civil rights equal treatment of minorities, including African Americans

democracy government that is run by its people

injustices things that are not fair

invaluable very worthwhile

promote to help something grow or get better

segregated separated from others

sutures threads used to sew up a wound